growing

Painz

Overcoming the STRUGGLE of SEXUAL PURITY
on the Path to Spiritual MATURITY

growing

Painz

Overcoming the STRUGGLE of SEXUAL PURITY
on the Path to Spiritual MATURITY

CIARRA LEATHERS

Kingdom Impactors Publishing
Houston, Texas
2014

Growing Painz: Overcoming the Struggle of Sexual Purity on the Path to Spiritual Maturity

Published by Kingdom Impactors Publishing
P. O. Box 35708
Houston, Texas 77235-5708
Printed in the United States of America
Phone: 281-552-8817
Website: www.kingdomimpactors.com

ISBN 978-0-9822334-1-2

The harder the challenge the greater the growth.

Unknown

Dedication

For all the women and men in the world
who embrace the pursuit of Christ!

CONTENTS

ACKNOWLEDGMENTS

A special thanks to my Heavenly Father for giving me the vision to write another book. I thank you for your guidance through this process. My thankfulness could never match your forgiveness. Thank you for loving, covering, and keeping me.

My three gems: my mother, Latonia, grandmother, Cloteal, and Aunt Carolyn for being my biggest supporters throughout my life. My love and appreciation for you three is deeper than I could ever express in words. I am grateful, humbled and blessed to have such amazing women in my corner.

My brother and sisters, Ryan, Latoya, Angel, and Shamille - each one of you has been such a blessing. Your encouragement has been remarkable. My nieces, Paris and Brandie, I love you!

My best friend, Michael Davis who has been an encouragement since day one, helping me with the pages of this book through many long nights and early mornings, I sincerely thank you. You are definitely my sunshine. I know our friendship is ordained and guided by God. I love you!

To my closest friends - Sisters and Brothers in Christ who were in my corner through it all, Nikeda Michelle, Gina Dimiceli, Ambriell Washington, Roseann Mattocks, William Hardrick, Jr., Solomon Bass, David Burney, and Chanita

Jones. Krislyn King, thank you for helping me through this last situation, you have shown yourself to be a true friend.

My new church family, RiverPointe Church and Pastor Patrick Kelley, thanks for welcoming me with open arms and covering me with an awesome Word each week.

Beacon Light SDA church where it all began. There is no place like the church that has shaped and poured in me for so many years. Thank you for your prayers from long distance. Thank you for always welcoming me, back home, with love and appreciation. Pastor Dr. Compton Ross and your wife, Mrs. Pamela Ross, thank you for the fruit you two continue to bear in my life and the encouragement and support you have shown. I love the Rosses.

Thank you, Mr. L. Randolph, Taleka Anderson, Johnathan Macklin, Elree Cantry, and Donna King for contributing to this book. Your continued support is appreciated. Also, thanks to the women who have allowed me to share their stories in the efforts to heal others.

I am grateful for Stephanie D. Miller, Dr. Bradley Smith, Bob Bergland, and Ann Thorne for your mentoring, correction, critics, and firm discipline with my writing. You have helped perfect my craft. Thank you for being patient with me over the years.

Lastly, a special, heart-felt thank you to my readers – you are loyal, supportive, and always encouraging me. Thank you for your support and emails, they do not go unnoticed. You are the best!

Thanks to the many that were not named, and know that I am thankful for the prayers, support, and love you have displayed. THANK YOU, and continued Blessings!

FOREWORD

My first encounter with Ciarra Leathers was in Houston, Texas when I went back to school in pursuit of an MA in counseling. We attended several classes together and were partnered together on class projects occasionally. I had completed my doctorate degree in Kansas City, Missouri and she had spent time growing up there so we had a connection and were able to discuss things we both had experienced in the area. We kept in touch after graduation and I have had the opportunity to watch her grow in many areas of her life to the point where she has been a blessing to many young ladies who struggle with identity, self-esteem, co-dependency and trust issues. Ciarra has not only studied these areas, but has experienced them in her own life. Her life has become a powerful testimony to the transforming power of Christ, as well as an encouragement to other ladies who encounter similar struggles. She displays a gripping transparency, empathy, reality and understanding of her personal struggles in her writing, which is seldom seen today. It is empowering to her readers. She continues on the path of discovery - understanding who she is and where she is going. She invites her readers on a journey of personal discovery, honesty, and transformation which is exciting and powerful.

When we focus on the hurt in our lives and allow anger and bitterness to take over, it is impossible to grow spiritually and be productive and successful in life. However, when we realize that God is sovereign and are able to view our circumstances from a new perspective, the healing process can begin. As we view life as a learning journey, we are able to have a new appreciation for the hurts and struggles we encounter. The journey is often much more important than the destination, but we do not have to journey alone. Let me encourage you to journey along with Ciarra through her writing, knowing that you are not alone in your struggle.

Rev. Dr. Bradley Smith, D.Min., M.Div., LPC
Houston, Texas

When I was a child, I spoke and thought and reasoned as a child does. But when I grew up, I put away childish things.
1 Corinthians 14:11 NIV

The further you run from your sins the more exhausted you are when they catch up to you.
Unknown

INTRODUCTION
TO GROWING PAINZ

As women, we seek to find love and happiness in whoever will show it. As men, we seek to find happiness at the moment, or sometimes for temporary pleasure. Some men want to love but were not shown the appropriate way to express love. Love is an action word not just a feeling; if we want to know how to effectively show and give love we have to know from where it resonates. My source for finding love was through my relationship with God; as it grew, I grew in the understanding of what love meant. Through my love for Him, He showed me the good, bad, and the UGLY of love. The good moments made me appreciate the bad and the ugly moments. It showed me that love is a process and it's a struggle. But if you are willing to sacrifice for it, it can be worth it. Someone once told me, you cannot truly appreciate love until you have been hurt before, and you can never fully understand love until you experience pain. Through a relationship with God you can learn how to effectively love and receive love through the pain. The strong exterior you have will start to soften and you will become more vulnerable, more accepting, more open, and see clearer- these will be your *growing painz*.

Overview of the Book

When you have experienced so much hurt in your life, it is difficult to grow spiritually. It is hard to recognize your own shortcomings because you have become affected by the pain of others and blinded to your own. I realized after many bad experiences with men that I could no longer blame my past. I had to accept responsibility for my own actions. Sometimes I take a glimpse at my future and see how I am allowing my past to still control it. Have I allowed myself to heal from past mistakes?

After writing *Season of Singleness* I moved forward, but the healing process was just beginning. I had to learn to love despite of being afraid. I had to understand that love in any relationship involves the risks of being hurt and being vulnerable. Sometimes it hurts, sometimes it's beautiful, but I would not know this unless I allowed myself to go through it. Christ sat amongst the worst, taking a chance, knowing His heart would be broken. Still He chose love, even when it was not reciprocated. That is the example that I choose to follow every day, even when it hurts, because Christ is sovereign.

During this healing process, I had to understand who and what I was allowing to pursue me. By allowing the Lord to pursue me, I was allowing Him to heal me from all of my misfortunes from prior bad relationships. Once I understood the true meaning of love, it no longer came in the form of lust, rather in the pursuit of Christ. My definition of love was no longer distorted, but changed. Now I view love as commitment rather than an emotional need.

Growing Painz will show how I struggled to form healthy relationships and deal with trust issues. This book will also show

how I overcame the generational curses of past hurts and entered a new covenant of receiving love, honoring love, and showing love. This book will take you through my life experiences of emotional hardships, entering relationships expecting the worse, always looking for a father in my relationships. *Growing Painz* will also walk you through other women's past hurts and their struggles while they wait for a husband and the lessons they have learned or the lessons they are in the process of learning. Each lesson was *painful* because they paid more attention to the wait rather than letting God mold that person He has for them. Instead, they rushed into relationships with persons who had no intentions of loving them.

Growing Painz is written from the female perspective based on my experiences and what I have witnessed in others. The ideas found in this book may not be everyone's truth, but it does apply to someone. My hope is it helps YOU!

Disclaimer: The names have been changed to conceal their true identities. At this printing, each is aware of this book being written to assist in the healing and deliverance of its readers.

CHAPTER ONE

A Hole That Needed to Be Filled

As a child growing up I had the love of a caring mother. My mother loved me dearly, but all the love she showed me could never amount to the pain I was going to experience by not having a father present. My interaction with a male figure was nonexistent. My mother did an excellent job taking on both roles as father and mother but the emotional need was still there. I longed for a male presence in my life and was not able to receive it. As I continued to have this need within, I searched for a man that would replace my father. The emotional need was so strong that it followed me throughout my life.

Let me take you back to my home environment. Growing up without a father was difficult because I believe the first man we, as women, are supposed to fall in love with is our fathers. That was not the case for me. Although I had a male presence in the home it was not the same. My mother's husband, my step father was physically present in the home, but not emotionally there. In addition, he had other children of his own to take care of - which he did. I needed a father to talk with, to confide in, to tell me how boys are trouble and mostly, how to meet the right boy. What I lacked was understanding and discernment. For me, there were no late night talks, no prep for meeting "jerks," no understanding that I would have my heart broken probably more than once and that it might be harder each time. I was never told that I would probably break hearts, too; that love has to be earned, not freely given that tears may come, but all tears are not from pain and one day I will learn from mistakes made. What I saw was the perpetuation of a generational curse, or deficit resulting in – *a hole that needed to be filled.*

Over time, I learned that my father's father was not in his life, so his life became a reflection of what he knew. My stepfather's father was not in his life, so he couldn't make the emotional connection because he was never shown how. An absent father to a daughter is one thing, but not to have it for a son is a whole different feeling. The love my father and stepfather did not receive in their homes made it extremely difficult for them to express it in their own household. My biological father's father was not in his life, so I could not expect him to understand the importance of being in mine. Although I once hated him for not loving me and showing me how to love others, I understand now. These two men who I wanted to learn from couldn't teach me anything because they were never taught. They never knew the importance of being **emotionally** there. They only knew abuse, betrayal, abandonment, and dysfunction. So how could I expect my biological father and my stepfather to master something they have never seen mastered? Sadly, dysfunction creates dysfunction.

As I grew up, I only saw the worst of men, both my grandpas were cheaters. I never saw a man who was faithful, who honored a woman, who honored and respected his children. My views on men were tainted from the beginning. I was unaware of the definition of an honorable man; I did not think they existed. This generational "curse" continues to manifest itself throughout many families; it is a curse that is prevalent in minority homes and is affecting our family system. It is important to have a traditional home environment with both parents actively present in the home.

Do not allow this *hole* to manifest itself within the safe haven of your home - break it by acknowledging how its presence affects you and those you love. Fill it with the One who can and should. Live wholly for your children and not out of your own emotional needs.

My biggest realization was the hole was not only emotional, but spiritual.

Let's look at some of the hole-filling ***painz*** I dealt with in my life.

Reflections on the Path to Spiritual Maturity

My personal take-way from this chapter (what impacted me most):

_____

_____

Favorite quote from this chapter:

_____

_____

Area(s) covered that I am strongest in:

_____

_____

Area(s) covered that I need to grow in:

_____

_____

Scriptures and other resources to study (use for journaling and prayer):

_____

_____

_____

Who I will ask to hold me accountable (list the actions needed):

_____

_____

_____

Who I can help (share the lessons learned with others who need them):

_____

_____

_____

CHAPTER TWO

Painz of Adulterous Spirit

My longing for a male emotional presence in my life was going to come crashing down. I met Troy at church through mutual friends. He was engaged at the time but the attraction was obvious when we were introduced. Although he couldn't get pass my tattoos, and piercing, being one of those *extremist* church folks. We soon would become really good friends. We had a lot in common, the same personality, the same drive, the same motivation, but most importantly the same love for Christ. After our first introduction, we continued to run into each other at church gatherings or friend's events and he would always find the time to talk to me. He would ask about my life, just to engage in small talk. I just thought he was a really nice guy, noisy, but nice.

Later, I went off to college and he got married. I would periodically come home for holidays, and run into him at church. He introduced me to his wife. We eventually changed numbers and kept in contact with each other, we talked often. His wife was aware of our conversations. Sometimes our conversations would last all night. Warning *painz!* I knew this interaction was not safe but I thought that since his wife was aware of our communication, then it was okay. I still could not deny my attraction to him. We both like being needed and he wanted to help me. Coming from an upbringing without a father, I enjoyed the attention from another male. We got "comfortable" with one another, not realizing the comfort was going to cause friction in our friendship and his marriage. We didn't know how to set boundaries and because of our lack of understanding, our friendship came to an end. I was upset and confused at first, but as I grew in my faith walk, I grew to accept that his decision was the right choice.

The painful truth was there were inappropriate acts by both of us that were disrespectful to his marriage. It was inappropriate to talk about my developed body parts, his detailed sexual relations with his wife, and his desire to engage in a threesome with him, his wife, and me. I was totally against the threesome but I enjoyed the attention I was receiving from Troy. What started out as an innocent friendship became dangerous. Although we never engaged in physical acts, the conversations were just as inappropriate. We needed to understand this. He needed to understand how to interact with a single woman, transitioning himself from a single man to a married one. I needed to understand that my unresolved issues, or hole, of not having a father present in my life were in play. Although I had good intentions, the needy part of me did not allow me to understand the sacredness of a covenant marriage union.

The end to our friendship was a ***growing painz***. I learned to effectively deal with my issues of not having a father in my life. I had to understand that I could no longer walk with guilt, playing the victim. I chose to accept the life that I did not have and make a new one, no longer being trapped in playing the blame game. I chose to live my life and be FREE of my past hurts.

Growth Points

- Setting boundaries in friendships is necessary, especially if your friend is married.
- If you have an attraction toward a married woman or man, it's probably safe not to be friends.
- Examine your motive for pursuing a relationship with a member of the opposite sex.
- When either side displays suspect behavior in violation of your morals and principles- **RUN!**
- Both parties should display appropriate behavior – that which is easily displayed, anytime, anywhere.
- Learn the honorable ways a man should interact with women other than his wife.
- Men, make sure your wife is comfortable with your female friend.
- Close the door on toxic people that are detrimental to your marriage
- Make wise decisions, especially when you first notice desires in your flesh – emotional and sexual.
- Always be willing to talk with your spouse about concerns in your marriage, not a friend of the opposite sex.
- Hold yourself accountable. You ultimately will have to work out your own issues with God.
- Make sure your friends have fellowship and/or relationship with your spouse.
- Late night calls with the opposite sex that is not your wife is **NEVER** appropriate.

- If an attraction is there, always talk with the person in the presence of your spouse.
- Be willing to examine certain reactions with people to see if it is beneficial to the relationship.
- Protecting your home and protecting your spouse is always the right thing to do.
- Males and females can be friends if the proper boundaries are set.
- A marriage union should be treated as sacred by both parties.
- Never defile, or dishonor your relationship by allowing a third party to enter.
- Communication is extremely important in a marriage. **Talk out the issues.** If it is difficult, seek professional help.
- An emotional connection with someone other than your spouse is a form of cheating.
- A marriage can still be mended and strengthened, even after infidelity.
- Restoring trust takes time after infidelity, but it can be done.
- Date nights are essential for a growing marriage. **Men**, it's important to continue the pursuit after the wedding.
- Love can be challenging, but the benefit and blessing is worth the sacrifice.

So you may be asking this question - *Where can someone find the appropriate view on love and marriage?* It starts with Christ!

Through my transitioning period I was able to grow in understanding of what love and friendship look like. Love is not always about actions, but the thought process in the action

- what you are not willing to do and the sacrifices you are willing to take to resist the desires of your flesh – emotional and sexual. When you love a person you do not take advantage of them. Although I thought Troy was helping me with my father issues, it was a hindrance to my spiritual growth, but I did not see that at the time. The respect we should have for our friendships with mankind and God should be bigger than our personal desires. It's okay to be available for your friend, but not in a way that will jeopardize their growth.

Transferring my love for God toward a man was another indication of *painz*. The attention I was longing for was always for Christ, but I had to go through the situation with Troy to understand that only He could fill the hole in my heart. What I thought was my longing for Troy was actually my longing for God. An emotional and spiritual affair had already begun in our hearts, although our friendship started so innocently. It had the potential to become more dangerous, if Troy had not cut off communication. Through my confusion and more so my healing, I was able to fall back in love with God. Troy was only a glimpse of what I desired from God - attention. Although God had always shown me attention, it took me a while to notice it and to be satisfied with it. Although I learned this late, eventually I was able to walk away, and grow.

Now, let's look at one of the subtle, but more dangerous *growing painz* – pride.

Reflections on the Path to Spiritual Maturity

My personal take-way from this chapter (what impacted me most):

_____

_____

Favorite quote from this chapter:

_____

_____

Area(s) covered that I am strongest in:

_____

_____

Area(s) covered that I need to grow in:

_____

_____

Scriptures and other resources to study (use for journaling and prayer):

_____

_____

_____

Who I will ask to hold me accountable (list the actions needed):

_____

_____

_____

Who I can help (share the lessons learned with others who need them):

_____

_____

_____

CHAPTER THREE

Painz of Pride

Pride goes before destruction, a haughty spirit before a fall.
Proverbs 16:18 NIV

O ften times we allow pride to take over our lives unconsciously. We think we have everything under control when we really do not. My poor decision to grow feelings for a married man was an act of pride. Not understanding the feelings I had for him was only because he showed me the attention for which I longed, felt I needed, longed for since I was a little girl and did not receive from my father.

There is a story in the Bible that helped me understand how harmful pride can be. In Joshua 7:3-5, Joshua and the Israelites first went after Ai, a small city east of Bethel, and Achan, a member of one of the tribes of Israel sinned and broke the covenant he made with God. He stole something that God commanded him to take away and destroy. The effects of his sin were not only felt by the Israelites but his family. Achan did not take God's commands seriously and it resulted in his own destruction. My actions, like Achan's, affected more people than me, it affected Troy's wife. My desire to hold on to **painz** of my pride, rather than destroy the unhealthy relationship I had with Troy, almost caused my own personal and spiritual destruction. Pride is present when we hold onto people and things that we know are not permissible or best for us. I learned I will never overcome the *spirit* of pride until I remove it first in every area of my life. (Joshua 7:12-13 NIV)

The attention I was seeking to fill the hole in my heart was *with me* all along. Even though I had heard about God, I did not know Him. I had yet to experience his presence in my life until I had died to my fleshly desires to experience and truly know the *need* for Him in my life. Now, every time I am tempted to relapse, I am reminded of Achan.

Reflections on the Path to Spiritual Maturity

My personal take-way from this chapter (what impacted me most):

_____

_____

Favorite quote from this chapter:

_____

_____

Area(s) covered that I am strongest in:

_____

_____

Area(s) covered that I need to grow in:

_____

_____

Scriptures and other resources to study (use for journaling and prayer):

_____

_____

_____

Who I will ask to hold me accountable (list the actions needed):

_____

_____

_____

Who I can help (share the lessons learned with others who need them):

_____

_____

_____

CHAPTER FOUR

Pains of Self-Imposed Rules

The reason I continued to go through the issues involving men in my life is because I continued to choose the same type of guy - even in friendships. I had a *rule* in play and I never detoured from it. The rough exterior I was familiar with had only been the cause of hurt in my life. That facade distorted my perception of what love could really be. My attempt at control was operating in a way that love was a set of rules and regulations I had to follow. Those rules included writing a list hoping I would find love by my specifications. Surely if I jotted down what I wanted in a man, he will come sooner than later.

My rules continued to get me hurt, because I did not consult God, but relied instead on my list and not God's plan for my life. Going into a relationship without fully addressing my issues was the start of an impending disaster. Honestly - how can I fully engage myself in another person when I am not sure about myself yet?! My rules were selfish, only intended to please my wants and desires. My rules never had God in them. Although I wrote them with pure intentions, but without the guidance of God, pure intentions become selfish ambitions. My understanding of rules was falsified by my upbringing. I did not know the meaning of true love until I fully engaged with Christ.

Having a list is not bad in itself, but it will only slow down the process of how God will use you. You cannot listen to God when you are walking in your own way. Listening is absorbing and accepting God's way. Learning understands the implications He is giving you and obedience is putting into action all we have learned. Self-imposed rules were my ***growing painz.***

My rules didn't reflect my life in Christ. They only *hindered* it.

Reflections on the Path to Spiritual Maturity

My personal take-way from this chapter (what impacted me most):

_____

_____

Favorite quote from this chapter:

_____

_____

Area(s) covered that I am strongest in:

_____

_____

Area(s) covered that I need to grow in:

_____

_____

Scriptures and other resources to study (use for journaling and prayer):

_____

_____

_____

Who I will ask to hold me accountable (list the actions needed):

_____

_____

_____

Who I can help (share the lessons learned with others who need them):

_____

_____

_____

CHAPTER FIVE

Painz of Confusing Love, Like and Lust

Love, like, and lust are very different. Although we may claim to be in love, some of us are actually overcome by lust.

> *Love is patient; **[like is semi-patient; lust requires immediate sexual satisfaction]**. Love is kind, **[like is semi-kind; lust is harsh]**. Love does not demand its own way; **[lust does]**.*
>
> ### *1 Corinthians: 13:4 NIV*
> [with author's editorializing]

For many women love, like, and lust are distorted. We often believe if sexual intercourse is involved that the person must love me. The truth of the matter is that sexual intercourse distorts your perception of what real love is. Yes, the act of sexual intercourse is biblical, but it is designed to bring two people together as one flesh, a deeply spiritual connection that ties you to that person for life. Sex was intended for a marriage union.

Society has made it normal to engage in sex before marriage. This does not make it right. No sex before marriage should still be practiced. The complication of having sex before marriage distorts your emotional state. It causes you to intertwine love with like and to settle for lust. If your own issues have not been properly addressed, it brings about disconnect and unfilled holes in your relationships. That is one reason a lot of people are together who should not be together. They are solely basing their connection through an emotional soul tie and/or sex without investigating the root of the connection to see if the emotion matches the truth.

Lastly, lust treats sex as an isolated physical act rather than an act of commitment to the person you love. Outside of marriage, sex destroys relationships. Inside marriage, it builds a strong connection between you and your spouse. Lust can be persuasive, especially when it takes on a false image of "love." Remember, true love should not go against devotion, honor and the truth of God's Word.

In the next section, let's read the accounts of other people who experienced their own *growing painz* while pursuing true love.

Please note: The names have been changed to conceal their true identities. The women who shared their personal stories are in the healing process or are currently going through their situations while seeking spiritual guidance. If there are any similarities in any of your relationships, please seek Godly wisdom and find the courage to exit.

Reflections on the Path to Spiritual Maturity

My personal take-way from this chapter (what impacted me most):

_____

_____

Favorite quote from this chapter:

_____

_____

Area(s) covered that I am strongest in:

_____

_____

Area(s) covered that I need to grow in:

_____

_____

Scriptures and other resources to study (use for journaling and prayer):

_____

_____

_____

Who I will ask to hold me accountable (list the actions needed):

_____

_____

_____

Who I can help (share the lessons learned with others who need them):

_____

_____

_____

CHAPTER SIX

Kerry's Story

K erry has been alone much of her adult life. Every relationship prior to her 30's was never sufficient. She deeply longed for a companion, someone she could trust and share her life with. Every man Kerry ever trusted never intended to go further in the relationship. Through her search for the perfect man she ended up meeting losers and non-committers. After her last relationship lasted for three years and ended at age 33, she vowed to not engage in sexual activity until she knew the relationship was going somewhere. She did not give herself a timeline but she knew she did not want to give herself to another man without a serious commitment. She was turning 34 soon and still no marriage or children, she began to question if God had someone for her. She had given up on preparing herself in the wait. A group of her girlfriends decided to fly her out to Las Vegas for her 34th birthday to get her mind off things. She was not nearly as excited about the trip as her girlfriends were. Kerry had already planned to sit at home and mope around the house. Her girlfriends thought this trip was just what she needed to get her mind off of being single at 34.

The women arrived in Las Vegas on the night of Kerry's birthday and decided to walk the strip. They were Christian women, so the club scene was out. Walking along the strip, Kerry accidentally bumped into a man. He excused himself and was apologetic to her although she bumped into him. He offered to take her out sometime but she declined. The man, Dan, continued to talk to her and she eventually told him she was only in Las Vegas for a couple of nights for her birthday weekend. He was in Las Vegas, too, for the weekend and planned to return home to Texas. Ironically, Kerry was from Texas as well, so the two exchanged numbers and continued to hang out in Las Vegas with their friends. When arriving back to Texas, Kerry and Dan were inseparable. They talked on the phone every day and they went everywhere together. He seemed like the guy of her dreams, the man she'd always wanted and had been looking to pursue.

After two months of dating, Dan asked for her hand in marriage. She was ecstatic, in all the years of dating and having sexual relations with the men in the past, none had proposed marriage to her. Kerry immediately started planning her wedding. She started having sex with him the night he proposed marriage. She found a home for the two of them and signed her name on the dotted line. Dan had bad credit so he was unable to sign his name alongside hers. Things were going smoothly and she hired movers to move her possessions into the new home. Kerry found the perfect wedding dress online. She hired a wedding planner to organize her wedding. Things were looking up for Kerry, or so she thought.

Kerry had moved in completely when she noticed that Dan was acting differently. He had another house that he was renting out to a woman who he had prior relations with. He would stop by the previous woman's home often before coming home to her. Each time he would stay longer at his old place than before. Dan also became possessive, not wanting Kerry to leave the home without him. He always *needed* to know where she was and with whom. Her fairytale was turning into a nightmare right before her eyes. The wedding was approaching. Kerry had already paid for most of everything for the wedding. Invitations were sent out and people had already booked flights. Kerry wanted her relationship with Dan to work out so she ignored all the warning signs and continued on like nothing was happening.

Kerry desperately wanted to get married. So she ignored every warning sign placed in front of her. The wedding was one month away and everything that could go wrong went wrong. Some nights Dan would not come home and claimed that he was partying all night with the guys. He would take unexpected trips out of town without her

> *Women need to understand- just because a man is sent in your path does not mean he is from God.*

knowing beforehand. She suspected that he was cheating, but did not have solid proof. Kerry wanted to ask him about his behavior but was afraid of the reaction she would get. Finally, one day she muscled up enough courage to ask him after he came home "the next morning." Dan was furious at her accusations, and grabbed her arm and threw her with force to the ground. He then proceeded to throw things in her direction while angrily yelling at her. She lay on the ground with tears in her eyes, bruised, and fearful.

Kerry found herself in the middle of a dangerous situation with the man who proposed marriage to her. A man who claimed he loved her. Although Kerry forgot about God in the beginning and did not consult with him about marrying Dan,

God did not leave her. He was working, even in the midst of her disobedience. Surprisingly, there was a knock on the door. The neighbors had called the police. Apparently they heard yelling coming from Kerry's home. Dan was arrested and Kerry moved out of the home and called off the wedding.

Ponder Point: Distractions

Can you imagine that same incident happening to you? Kerry was so focused on not having someone in her life, she forgot about God. She focused on her life as a single woman rather than working on herself and her own issues. Kerry was only comfortable in relationship with someone, not by herself. She was so accustomed to being in a relationship that she forgot about herself. More so, she forgot about God. Kerry threw herself into building a life with Dan wishing instead of praying first. In hindsight, I believe that Dan was a test - a distraction from Kerry's purpose of loving and appreciating herself.

God's approval should always override ours. Often, we go in relationships hoping God will agree with our decisions instead of the other way around. Just because it may take years for some to get married does not mean anything is wrong with us. It means it is not our time. When, we, women completely understand and accept this, our eyes will be more widened to what God has for us instead of what we have for ourselves. Kerry knows that now.

Reflections on the Path to Spiritual Maturity

My personal take-way from this chapter (what impacted me most):

_____

_____

Favorite quote from this chapter:

_____

_____

Area(s) covered that I am strongest in:

_____

_____

Area(s) covered that I need to grow in:

_____

_____

Scriptures and other resources to study (use for journaling and prayer):

_____

_____

_____

Who I will ask to hold me accountable (list the actions needed):

_____

_____

_____

Who I can help (share the lessons learned with others who need them):

_____

_____

_____

CHAPTER SEVEN

April's Story

April recalls the morning she sat in her apartment, wondering how she was going to pay her rent. She was a full time hairstylist with four children. Some weeks her income was great and other weeks her income was low. The biological father of her four children was her ex-husband who was no longer in the children's lives since he could not be a part of hers. April was married for ten years before her relationship ended in divorce. They had been together since she was 13. Experiencing divorce was a painful time in her life. She felt like a failure. April did everything to make her marriage work, but she could not tolerate his constant infidelity. Marrying at the age of 19, love was unknown to her. Her divorce left a sour taste regarding relationships, her ex-husband was the only man she had known and loved. April's father was not present in her life. She was raised by her mother since her father left her mother before she was born. Her ex-husband was the "man void filler" for 16 years of her life - six years dating and ten years of marriage. After her marriage had ended, she had to be a responsible parent for her four children who needed her. April recognized her talents as a hairstylist and made that a career. Now that she was on her own with four children, she had to make sacrifices.

April did not have a solid relationship with Christ although she heard others speak of him. One day she was introduced to God by one of her clients and found peace and hope in the Lord through John 3:16. She was now a new believer and willing to understand and grow in God. After not being able to pay her rent, April was evicted and had to move in with her mother. She was bothered by the fact that she could not support her children and needed help. Instead of praying for all the answers, April again returned to her thought that being in a relationship was the answer to all her problems. She would randomly meet guys at night clubs and eventually started relationships with them. The dating scene was unfamiliar territory because most of her life had been spent with one man. A lot of the men she met did not want relationships, just casual sex. But, they would give her money which she accepted because she needed to support her children. Eventually, April moved out of her mother's home and into a house. Her boyfriend at the time would pay the rent as long as she kept up her "wifey" duties.

April cooked, cleaned, and had sex with him anytime he wanted. She was content with this life, because finally she was able to pay her living expenses and financially support her children. She rationalized this arrangement was all right because her children were fed and clothed. April even started going back to church with her

> *Wifey- IS NOT a wife. She is a woman you claim to care a lot about. One that is more than your girlfriend. She is your favorite, but not your only.*

boyfriend. Things were looking up for her until she came home from the hair shop one afternoon. Her boyfriend had completely moved out – with no explanation. No letter explaining why - just gone. April called his mother to see where he was. His mother was someone she had never met before, but she had the number only because he had used her phone to call her. His mother told April information she did not want to hear. Her boyfriend was married with three children. He and his wife were separated but they decided to work out their issues and get back together. April *supposedly* had no clue about his marriage. Although there were nights he would not come home because he claimed he was staying at his mother's house. The truth was the time he was away from her was spent attempting reconciliation with his wife. April was devastated and did not know how she was going to pay her bills. Eventually, she got a second job to maintain the house expenses.

After her breakup with her "boyfriend," April should have made God her #1 but she still tried to fill a void. She met another man on social media and started to communicate often. After a while, they exchanged numbers. April found out he was of a different religion than Christianity, what she was familiar with and still learning. Instead of parting ways with him, she decided to date him. Her foundation was not strong enough in the faith, leading her

> *Discovering the truth about marriages and other past relationships is a must! Separation does not equal divorce. If a man or woman is unhappy in their marriage, it does not give you the right to become involved.*

to make rash decisions. Soon, she converted to his religion and cut off all communication with her family and friends. April and her children moved into his home. As she continued to do hair on the side, one of her clients asked her why she would make such a permanent decision about her life and her children's lives.

She answered, "He bought me a new car, and I don't have to pay for anything but gasoline for my vehicle. He gave my children and me a place to live, rent free, and he showers me with gifts. I know I made the right decision."

Ponder Point: Conformity

April let her relationships with these different men take the place of God in her life. She continued to look for someone to fill this void in her life that started with her father. Her cry for attention and hurt was because of the first man that let her down - her father. The other men added to her wounds that were never healed. Instead, April's actions covered up her wounds with different men compounding the ***growing painz*** in the ten years spent with her ex-husband. April was unaware that she was living her life as a broken woman, with a wounded heart that never properly healed. She unconsciously allowed her past unresolved hurt from her father to close out the pursuit and love of God.

April had an insufficient covering of love, protection and support from her father and experienced the same with these other men in her life. April was never in the right place to start another relationship with any man. She needed to get in position to receive God's unfailing love before she could receive her blessing of her heart's desire. I believe her blessing will not be presented to her until she completely allows God to be her pursuit. April's wounds are ready to be healed, but she has to make the first steps toward healing. God is still waiting on April.

Reflections on the Path to Spiritual Maturity

My personal take-way from this chapter (what impacted me most):

_____

_____

Favorite quote from this chapter:

_____

_____

Area(s) covered that I am strongest in:

_____

_____

Area(s) covered that I need to grow in:

_____

_____

Scriptures and other resources to study (use for journaling and prayer):

_____

_____

_____

Who I will ask to hold me accountable (list the actions needed):

_____

_____

_____

Who I can help (share the lessons learned with others who need them):

_____

_____

_____

CHAPTER EIGHT

Natalie's Story

Natalie was a bright woman with a caring heart. She grew up in church and always had a desire to know more about God. She was married to a man she introduced to God and had three children. Natalie and Terry married for 4 years. But Natalie was still not use to submitting to his authority. Before she got married she was independent. Her early life: she practically raised her siblings. Her father and mother divorced when she was younger. She is very close to her father, even more than with her mother. Natalie had a huge responsibility when she was younger to take on raising two siblings when she was a child herself. When she became an adult, her mentality never shifted. When she met Terry, her biggest challenge was submitting to his leadership. They would have fights over the smallest matters-such as what to cook for dinner.

Terry's background was different. He came from a two-parent home with only one sibling- a sister. He had a close relationship with both of his parents and saw how effective his parents' marriage was. His mother was a stay-at-home mom and his father worked two jobs and when he would arrive from work, his dinner was already prepared along with a nice bath. Clothes were washed and ironed for his next day at work, and the house was orderly. Date nights were every weekend since his father was off on the weekends. They would set aside time after date night to talk about her needs and wants. The weekends were basically dedicated to her since the weekdays were dedicated to him. The arguments were rare in their household. They rarely argued around Terry. Periodically, the father would bring home unexpected gifts for his wife. This was the relationship Terry wanted for him and Natalie.

Their marriage was just the opposite; in the beginning they had fights about boundaries and how to establish them in a new union. One of Natalie's closes friends was male. Terry did not mind her having a male friend as long as he understood the boundaries of their relationship. Natalie thought as long as they were both monogamist in the marriage that the marriage would work. What she had to grow to understand was that a covenant relationship requires sacrifices and is more complex than monogamy. She had to submit to her husband even if she did not feel like doing so.

Natalie's upbringing was broken. She never had a positive outlook on a marriage relationship. She thought marriage was 50/50 after growing in her Word. She found out marriage is more 70/30. A wife has to submit first to God and then her husband and children. Natalie's view was backwards; she thought her children came before anybody, including God. She had to understand that God gave her a husband and then blessed her with children. Children are a blessing from God and also should be a bond that brings both husband and wife closer together, not divided. Natalie almost cost herself her marriage by not willing to submit to her husband and swallow her pride. She almost let her pride get in the way of a beautiful union. The one thing that was supposed to bind them together, Natalie almost let it tear them apart.

Two people from opposite backgrounds were joined together but why did it seem nearly impossible for the two to stay together? Maybe a better question is: What does it take to keep a marriage flourishing despite the disagreements? A marriage relationship has to be looked at as the covenant we are joined to by God. Just as our relationship with God is built on His love and commitment toward us despite our actions, so a marriage relationship is designed to be just as solid. Although Natalie and Terry's marriage was headed for divorce, they were able to save their marriage by both agreeing to make it work. The commitment Terry made to his wife was stronger than the disagreements. Instead of letting their arguments divide them, they decided to work through them. I am happy to say Natalie and Terry's marriage relationship is now much stronger.

Marriage in God's eye is a lifelong covenant, one of the greatest gifts you could share with another person. It can also be the greatest pain you will ever go through in life. Marriage is solely based on a commitment to one another, not emotions. The choice is ultimately yours to make. Every marriage is not like Natalie and Terry's, but the foundation should be the same. You two are both fighting and working towards growth and becoming more and more like Christ –as individuals and as a unit.

Ponder Point: Submission or Independence

We must first submit to God and then the problems involving submission to others will be resolved by Him. Let's take a closer look.

First, submission is an attitude and NOT just an action. Submission begins in the heart. Many times people who claim to be submissive are only outwardly going through the motions of submission, while inwardly, they are still resenting their position in life. If you find yourself in the position where being submissive is difficult for you, a prayer is in order.

> *Father, help me to be content in the role as a wife/ husband and give me a submissive spirit, not only toward my husband/wife but also toward members in the body of Christ. Let me be an example of how Christ was when He walked the earth. Let me serve, and not expect to be served. In Jesus' name I pray, Amen.*

Second, independence is not for married people. Independence in a relationship implies you have no desire to be *joined* with another person. (Genesis: 24 NIV) Independence allows pride to lead you into ruin. Many times those who claim to be independent fear the thought of being dependent on someone else. Walking with Christ is all about being dependent on Him and dying to self – conforming your very actions and thoughts to those that are like Christ. In order to grow in submission to Him, being dependent on Him is a must. A reversal of being an independent woman, when married, is necessary.

The 7 things Natalie learned while going through her tough transition from independence to submission are:

1. Let go of pride in order to allow God to use you.
2. Have a genuine friendship with your spouse.
3. Accept your spouse's flaws and encourage his efforts.

4. Laugh with your spouse.
5. Show your appreciation by honoring him/her.
6. Find new ways to love them, and keep your relationship fresh.
7. Make sure the time between saying "I love you" is short.

Reflections on the Path to Spiritual Maturity

My personal take-way from this chapter (what impacted me most):

_____

_____

Favorite quote from this chapter:

_____

_____

Area(s) covered that I am strongest in:

_____

_____

Area(s) covered that I need to grow in:

_____

_____

Scriptures and other resources to study (use for journaling and prayer):

_____

_____

_____

Who I will ask to hold me accountable (list the actions needed):

_____

_____

_____

Who I can help (share the lessons learned with others who need them):

_____

_____

_____

CHAPTER NINE

No Guy or Girl Code – Yes, the God Code

Most mistakes we learn from are the ones we create. We are not bound by a societal code often identified as the "guy or girl code," but rather by a code written and established by God. People cheat because of sin. Men do because they are often taught by societal codes to obtain women, not love women. When we start listening to society rather than God, it produces temptation. Temptation produces sin. Sin produces death. Temptation is the inclination to, or beginning of sin. It begins with an evil thought and becomes sin when we dwell on the thought. Eventually, the thought become an action.

What does this look like in practice? The codes of society say it is all right to flirt with a single woman or single man when you are married. What is perceived as innocent behavior will not go further than a flirt. However, looking back and assessing your position as a spouse, you can see how detrimental flirting could be. It not only leads the single or married person on, but gives them hope for something more.

~67~

Gentlemen, you will not be dishonoring the guy code if you respect your marriage and consider your marriage top priority over your fleshly desires. No matter how attractive or interesting the conversation is with a single woman, God has already formed your spouse for you and gave you a commandment to love her like Christ loves His church.

> *Husbands, love your wives, even as Christ also loved the church and gave himself for it.*
> **Ephesians 5:25 NIV**

Women, no matter what you see in a man that you do not see in your husband, your husband will always hold precedence over that single man. God does not make mistakes, so the man he designed for you is right where he needs to be-*with you.* The temporary fulfillment with another man will soon fade. If you are not receiving the attention you need from your husband get it from God. Seek God for fulfillment, and stay in His presence when you feel the need for extra attention.

> *Wives, submit yourselves to your own husbands as you do to the Lord. For the husband is the head of the wife as Christ is the head of the church, His body, of which He is the Savior. Now as the church submits to Christ, so also wives should submit to their husbands in everything.*
> **Ephesians 5:23-24 NIV**

Gentlemen and women, no matter what you are going through in your relationships, your circumstances are never so bad that you should bring another person into it. It is never beyond God's help. Remember, Sarah was able to have a child after she thought she was barren and gave her servant Hagar to her husband, Abraham. Job received a new family after losing everything and we are able to have our shortcomings forgiven because Christ chose to pay. Because we belong to a loving God, we need never to despair. We never know what good He will bring out of a seemingly hopeless situation, if we trust Him despite how things appear to us.

Too often we rely on our own strength instead of trusting God. We go to God only when obstacles seem too great. However, consulting God, even when we "think" we are capable may save us from grave mistakes. God may want us to learn lessons and remove the spirit of pride before He will work in us and through us. When things seem too hard, you can always seek the counsel of trained Godly professionals or clergy for additional support.

Reflections on the Path to Spiritual Maturity

My personal take-way from this chapter (what impacted me most):

_____

_____

Favorite quote from this chapter:

_____

_____

Area(s) covered that I am strongest in:

_____

_____

Area(s) covered that I need to grow in:

_____

_____

Scriptures and other resources to study (use for journaling and prayer):

_____

_____

_____

Who I will ask to hold me accountable (list the actions needed):

_____

_____

_____

Who I can help (share the lessons learned with others who need them):

_____

_____

_____

CHAPTER TEN

Emotional Growth: Gaining the Strength to Say NO

In my past relationships with men, I believed that meeting *the one* would be the perfect ending to what had been a sad beginning in my life. Deep down inside, a woman knows what is best for her, even though she may not act accordingly. My heart caused me to refuse being with someone to make another person happy. Settling and rushing the wait because others thought that I should be married was NOT an option. As my relationship with Christ continues to grow today, I have a greater understanding of the dynamics of a marriage relationship. Marriage is not something you rush into. You don't marry someone out of fear, loneliness, fulfillment, affirmation, or wholeness. Christ has fulfilled all of the voids that I once had. Another person entering my life will only *add* to what God has already completed. **Lesson learned: *a man does not complete you, Christ does.*** Once I often wondered whether God has someone for me. Now, I've discovered that the one man I've been longing for is God. Not until my relationship was solid with Him, another person entering my life would have been a distraction – and *not* my husband. In reflection, I know that every man that entered my life was a part of my *growing process.* I said NO because they were not the one. Their wives were out there waiting for them. It wasn't me - or my time.

Next, I will share accounts of two men in my life that others thought was the one, even me.

Jerold

Jerold entered my life unexpectedly. We had no intention of becoming anything but friends, although our attraction for each other was obvious. We had a lot in common and the love we both had for Christ was amazing. We both desired God to work in our lives. Even the steps we were willing to take to make God's presence evident in our lives were the same. The bulk of our conversations were focused on our walk with Christ and what we both could do to strengthen it. From the beginning, we were both vocal about our faith, and our lives in Christianity. We both saw eye-to-eye on the same subject matters pertaining to the Body of Christ. As our friendship grew, we both longed for more than just conversation.

The relationship had started off as a friendship and grew into something more. We would talk often when we saw each other at school. The conversations were so impactful that even after class we would go grab a cup of tea/coffee and continue the conversation at a diner. We craved each other's conversation. The relationship seemed to work. We talked so much about the Body of Christ we never actually got to know one another individually. We eventually exchanged phone numbers, and our first conversation on the phone was interesting, but not as impactful as when we were in each other's presence. Eventually the phone conversations didn't last, he preferred to see me and talk in person. I agreed!

At the time, my relationship with God was in a growth spurt. I was still trying to be obedient in my walk. Meeting Jerold was different because we actually hit it off as friends first. He was single and so was I. There was nothing sexual that had occurred on either side. We never so much as hugged. The only physical contact was strictly handshakes. I started to tell my friends about Jerold and how our faith intertwined. My friends were excited about Jerold and immediately thought he was the one I've been waiting for. For the moment, I thought so, too.

Eventually that thought would be shaken during the next conversation we had. After class we both decided to get something to eat not too far from the school. We talked about our personal lives and what he wanted to do after graduation. What I learned rocked my world. Jerold was recently divorced after 8 years of marriage. His wife decided to end their marriage. There had been infidelity on his side. The two of them shared three children together. This did not include his three other children by different women, conceived before and during his marriage.

As I learned about all these women in his life, I also learned that he did not have a close relationship with his mother. Throughout his life, he was searching for fulfillment in these women. He was searching for the love of his mother. Even with his children, his four daughters, he was still learning how to love and express love. He did not want to be the father that his mother was to him. Although the love for his mother never ceased, he wanted that connection even in his adult life. He wanted answers. More importantly, he wanted love.

There was a look on my face, which surprised even me. I never like to hold anyone's past against them. How could I? We all have sinned and fallen short of God's glory. Anyone is able to repent and turn to a new way of living. That night, I looked deeply into his eyes and saw pain. He was looking for a transition. He had endured pain his whole life. I was actually honored that he chose to share some of his most private, painful, personal life with me. He revealed in the midst of all of his hardships, God planted in his heart to start a church. I was supportive, and wanted to be by his side to see this come full circle. His testimony was powerful and I knew he would reach a lot of people. Other men needed to hear how he survived these hardships in his life.

Jerold was skeptical about sharing his most inner private life with me because I was a woman and he was afraid that I would judge him and leave. He was afraid that I would walk out of his life like every other woman had done. He told me he felt comfortable enough to open up to me because he sincerely thought I could have been *the one*. He felt calm and relaxed around me, something he had not felt with another woman in a while. I continued to talk with Jerold and encourage him but I was still dealing with my own inner battles with my desires and issues of abandonment. Realistically, I was not ready to be a wife and first lady with six step children. I was still learning how to overcome my selfishness and how to love and appreciate me - by myself. To add others to that was not what I needed. As a result, I distanced myself from him because I knew I was not what his heart was searching for. My role was to be a listening ear - only.

The distance hurt me, but I knew it was best for both of us. In the middle of my pain, I experienced **emotional growth.**

Then I received a text!

Jerold: *It's just like a woman to stop calling you or answering your text. You are a wonderful woman and I only wish your husband the best because I know what he has. God Bless!*

Me: *I hope you did not take my distance as abandonment, which is the last thing I want you to feel. However, there are times in a person's life when you have to release what doesn't belong to you. Moving forward in this transition you're about to take has "wait" requirements and I believe that this is your Season of growth. You are already well on your way. You decided to trust and move on God's accord and not your own. I'm still learning that, Jerold. I'm in a transitional period, to condition my mind so I can be effective spiritually. You are going to make some woman happy one day and I will be there to cheer you on. I'm just not her. Blessings, Jerold!*

Some readers may think that Jerold was my husband. I thought so, too, but God told me he was not. You cannot go into a relationship with unresolved issues. I was still dealing with mine. We both were. We were too much alike - struggling with the same demon. We were not strong together, but were stronger apart. In order for growth to take place, one must realize the areas where growth is needed. We, as women, so badly want to be committed, that sometimes we make rash decisions based on emotions or spur-of-the-moment feelings. You have to be willing to deal with your unresolved issues that are lingering from your childhood or bad relationships before your husband finds you. I knew Jerold was *not* my husband because my issues were still being worked through. Timing is important.

Today, two years later, Jerold is married to a beautiful woman who appreciates his past and compliments his future. He found the type of love he needed but that I could not give. His wife gives that and more. Pastor Jerold has started his own church like God instructed him to do. His wife is over the Women's ministry and she co-parents his six beautiful children.

Carl

After my relationship with Jerold, I graduated and started focusing on growth and writing. During my journey I met Carl at a gathering. He was a man of God and we shared the same friends. We hit it off pretty quickly as friends. He was interested in me helping him with his business as an entrepreneur. I was willing to help him with what I knew of entrepreneurship. We began to have daily meetings to map out his vision of where he wanted to see himself in the next year or so. Carl was still in school working on his Masters. We were both pretty busy but managed to make time for each other regarding work and his vision. After working with Carl for a few months on his business providing pointers to help it further excel, he invited me to a barbeque at his cousin's house. Not thinking too much about the invitation, I decided to go. We both decided to drive separate cars. When I arrived at his cousin's house, I was introduced to his grandmother, uncles, cousins and mother. Talk about an awkward moment. I was so not prepared for that or what was next.

Apparently, Carl always had a crush on me. He wanted to see if I was interested in dating him. My first thought was *no* because he was not my type. I was not even remotely attracted to him physically. More so, I never looked at him any way other than as a nice guy. Then, I had a flashback of my friends telling me that I needed to stop dating the same type of man. Rather, look at the heart as God looks at our hearts. So I decided to date him. I entered into a relationship with someone I wasn't attracted to -not a good idea, for me. Because he was sweet, caring, loving, and loved Christ, I continued to date him. We differed on our interpretation of the Bible. For example, Carl believed that once you are divorced, you cannot get married again, even if your spouse commits adultery or has a baby outside the marriage. I disagreed, the Bible firmly states that there are validations for a divorce, one being infidelity. (Matthew 19:7-9) Although God frowns upon divorce and wants you to stay within the marriage and work through it, if both parties are not willing, my belief is that you can no longer stay in a marriage that is not working. Carl was very strong in his position when it came to his interpretation of the Word. He was strict and concise. Something about his convictions drew me closer to him.

The relationship continued with movie and dinner dates. Carl seemed like the perfect fit, but I still was not attracted to him physically. After six months of dating we still did not kiss. The lack of physical attraction did not allow me to - although he tried. I always managed to make up an excuse such as I was waiting for marriage to kiss again. Yes, it was horrible of me to lie, but it was either that or tell him the truth and hurt his feelings. This man really cared for me.

Then, a lesson was learned. The mere mention of marriage gave him the incentive to move forward in approaching me with the idea. I liked being around him, and by this time I was on a new level with God, moving forward and working through my issues. I said to God, "I think this is what I want. I'm leery, but I know my picks haven't been the best for me and maybe you have sent this guy in my life because he's unlike all the rest of the men I've dealt with. He has a heart for you and he treats me like a queen. If he asks for my hand in marriage, show me what I should do." I welcomed the idea of marriage with him but told him I was not sure if I was ready. Yes, I enjoyed spending time with him and really liked him, but it was not time to commit to marriage.

Still feeling uneasy, we began to move forward with our relationship. I was conflicted - happy but not really happy. I was happy because I enjoyed being around him. But, I was unhappy because I was not attracted to him like I thought I should be. By then, the lack of attraction went beyond the physical to other areas. When I conferred with a friend on the phone, she assured me that it was just nerves and that I wasn't used to someone like him. "Give it time," she said. Finally, the day came to ask me *the question*. He planned this elaborate dinner at one of my favorite restaurants. After we ate, he told me how he felt about me - the joy I bring to his life, the amazing moments we have shared together, and the strides I continue to take in my walk with Christ. Still, at that moment I had no clue of what was to come until he got down on one knee in the restaurant. People were watching and pointing. I was so embarrassed. How will I tell this man NO in front of all these people, especially when he had obviously thought this through?

Realizing at that moment that my heart and mind were saying NO I knew I had to tell him the truth. So I politely said, "I'm not ready." He was shocked, but he understood and said, "Well, when you are, I will be here." I could no longer string him along and pretend we had a future together when it was obvious to me that we did not. It wasn't my moment - again. I knew in my heart that his *true* wife was preparing herself for him and I just wasn't her.

I said **NO** to Carl's proposal solely because he was *not* my husband. I knew this because:

1) **The physical attraction wasn't there.**
   My desire and attraction for *other* men grew while I was with him. If you are going into a relationship and you are not attracted to the other person, it only heightens your chances of cheating. Physical attraction is important as is mental attraction. Humans naturally are visual people. However, physical imperfections can disappear if other strong qualities are present.

2) **I wasn't totally sold on him as a mate.**
   This should be the easiest decision you make. I hesitated long enough to know my head and heart were saying the same thing - **NO**.

3) **I wasn't ready.**
   Emotionally, I wasn't wowed by him. Mentally, I felt it was forced. The timing was wrong. We had a semblance of chemistry, but, for all the wrong reasons.

4) **I wasn't growing as a person with him.**
Carl was a comforter - not a motivator. I felt comfortable around him, but not enough to be motivated to grow. He never motivated me to become more than what I already was. However, I motivated him to grow. He could never push me to my full potential.

5) **I was not happy.**
Looking back, I was going through the motions with him. My happiness came from finally being with someone – not from the relationship itself. We had an emotionally-led relationship, not logically thought out. Carl had the ability to lead but we were going in opposite directions.

After the fact, I realize that Carl's heart was pure and his intentions were straight forward. I just was not the person with whom he was supposed to spend the rest of his life. Now that time has passed, Carl and I are cordial, although we don't talk often. He is dating and traveling the world as he ventures out as an entrepreneur.

Reflections on the Path to Spiritual Maturity

My personal take-way from this chapter (what impacted me most):

_____

_____

Favorite quote from this chapter:

_____

_____

Area(s) covered that I am strongest in:

_____

_____

Area(s) covered that I need to grow in:

_____

_____

Scriptures and other resources to study (use for journaling and prayer):

_____

_____

_____

Who I will ask to hold me accountable (list the actions needed):

_____

_____

_____

Who I can help (share the lessons learned with others who need them):

_____

_____

_____

CHAPTER ELEVEN

Before Saying - I DO

A well-known practice is rushing into relationships without considering everything because we are tired of being single. We may even realize the need to grow in the same areas. We are tired of the same relationship failures. My belief is that God allows certain events to happen in our lives to accomplish His overall purpose, but we are still responsible for our actions. Before you take action or allow another person of the opposite sex in your life, know your prior circumstances and be truthful about your motives. Ask yourself, "Am I sure God wants me to do this, or do I just want his approval on what I've decided to do anyway?"

While you wait to hear God's voice, here are things to consider before taking the next step in a relationship. If he or she can master the following then they can master what is needed to say "**I DO.**" They can and will:

- Be open to correction and direction from God.
- Respect *your* decision not to have premarital sex and will not put you in tempting positions to alter your commitment.

- Respect and honor their parents.
- Respect the leadership of others.
- Respect themselves. **It's all about respect**.
- Pray for you *and* with you.
- Motivate you to become better.
- Compliment and bolster your confidence – even if you feel you are not.
- Be willing to read the Word with you and by themselves to ensure their relationship with Christ is sufficient.
- Know and understand what love is and looks like through Christ.
- Not be egotistical, self-absorbed, or selfish.
- Make time for what they view as important no matter what.
- Communicate effectively.
- Realize that text messages are not a sufficient form of communication.
- As a man, has the confidence to lead a household - financially, physically, and with emotional stability.
- As a woman, has the desire to encourage, support, love, follow, and take care of her spouse's physical needs.

Reflections on the Path to Spiritual Maturity

My personal take-way from this chapter (what impacted me most):

_____

_____

Favorite quote from this chapter:

_____

_____

Area(s) covered that I am strongest in:

_____

_____

Area(s) covered that I need to grow in:

_____

_____

Scriptures and other resources to study (use for journaling and prayer):

_____

_____

_____

Who I will ask to hold me accountable (list the actions needed):

_____

_____

_____

Who I can help (share the lessons learned with others who need them):

_____

_____

_____

CHAPTER TWELVE

The Mission: Pursuing Spiritual Growth

It is so easy to search for fulfillment in things or a person. The challenge is pursuing spiritual growth in Christ. By doing so, you may find things out about yourself that you absolutely hate. There is a need for growth. In doing so, your actions will then bring about the results you want. You are responsible for your own growth – not another person. You are responsible for the decisions you make without consulting God. So regardless of what you have done in the past, you can start today with a new mindset, a new vision, and a new mission.

Relationships with people fail because we are flawed; we make mistakes, hurt people and harbor pride. Even after exiting a relationship that was not in God's will, we should still be gracious, and learn from the failure. The ending is not the hurtful part. The *consequences* of the ending were often painful – but, necessary for growth. Consequences are important to consider as we learn not to react from emotion and burn bridges as we exit. In some circumstances, it is probable that you will need to use that bridge again for friendships, support, help, encouragement, and growth. It is not wise to harbor resentment when consequences are the direct cause of your actions. Instead, accept the consequences of your actions, learn the lessons and move forward - in love. In order to do this you must forgive, which is a HUGE part of spiritual growth.

What are some benefits of Spiritual Growth for Christians who experience and embrace it?

- Growth in your relationship with Christ.
- Power to execute the sin of pride.
- Ability to forgive those who have wronged you.
- Forward movement in life - without resentment.
- A life led by logic and not by emotions.
- Hearing God's voice clearer than before.
- Focus on change and the renewal of your heart and mind.
- Acceptance of what you cannot change and a walk in newness.
- Fellowship with other believers that is different and rewarding.
- A new meaning of worship.
- Relationships with others that is no longer judgmental, but loving.
- Happiness for others who have hurt you.
- Freedom from harboring feelings of envy or pride.
- Constant contribution to the improvement of the Body of Christ.
- Continual personal growth in Christ.
- Finding fulfillment in Christ alone.

Reflections on the Path to Spiritual Maturity

My personal take-way from this chapter (what impacted me most):

_____

_____

Favorite quote from this chapter:

_____

_____

Area(s) covered that I am strongest in:

_____

_____

Area(s) covered that I need to grow in:

_____

_____

Scriptures and other resources to study (use for journaling and prayer):

_____

_____

_____

Who I will ask to hold me accountable (list the actions needed):

_____

_____

_____

Who I can help (share the lessons learned with others who need them):

_____

_____

_____

CHAPTER THIRTEEN

Growing In Christ

O ver the years, I have learned that focusing on pleasing God, rather than pleasing Ciarra, has made my life better. The direction God is leading me in is much better than the path I set out for myself. Yes, I tried being happy with a man. Fulfillment did not come. I tried being happy with things. Fulfillment did not come. I even tried being happy by myself - without God. Fulfillment did not come. Today, I notice I still need Christ to grow. So, I am totally surrendering, giving Him everything - even my current and past hurts. I want to *completely* grow. That requires obedience, discipline, and hard work. Therefore, I am willing to sacrifice everything my flesh – my mind, will and emotions – want and desire in order to begin walking *new* - in Christ. The great thing about being *in Christ* is my ending. Although my start was not pleasant, I no longer have thoughts of feeling undeserving, unworthy, or worthless because God sees me as He saw His prodigal son-**Worthy!**

In the story of the prodigal son, there is a conflict between the father and his other son who remained at home. The father was overjoyed that his prodigal, or lost son came back home.

However, the son who remained at home despised his brother's return with judgment and ridicule. We do that often within the Body of Christ. We see other's faults and we're quick to cast judgment instead of becoming a beacon of light welcoming them back. This does not mean we should ignore wrongdoing, but we no longer *see* their mistakes. When the prodigal returned home- all was forgiven. The difference between judgment and joy is our capacity to forgive.

We had to celebrate and be glad, because this brother of yours was dead and is alive again; He was lost and is found.
Luke 15:32 NIV

Jesus Christ's Sacrifice

We are all sinners and because of our sinful nature, we are incapable of pleasing God. As Paul puts it, those sinful people "dead in our sins" cannot please God. We needed someone who did not see us as we saw ourselves as sinners, doomed to die. Before Jesus, we deserved death. Jesus, by virtue of His sinless life paid the price on the cross. But God took the wrath we deserved and placed it upon Jesus Christ. He, who is perfect without sin- took on our sins- every lie, adulterous spirit, cheating habit, disgusting thought or action and became sin. The sacrifice of Jesus Christ is beyond human comprehension. He became sin - *our sin*- to rescue us from our filth. Jesus received the punishment our sins deserved. On the cross, He died. By His blood, we were made *right* with God. Jesus took our place, our debt, our punishment and made it His. What a God we serve! His love rescued us.

Jesus' sacrifice on the cross should be enough to fulfill us. We will not always have good thoughts and actions. However, if we are listening to God and following His lead, we will grow daily. We change daily to grow in Christ. Although change may be slow, it will happen if we trust God and are determined to grow in Him – His ways, thoughts and will for our lives.

> *God made Christ who had no sin to be sin for us, so that in Him we might become the righteousness of God.*
> **2 Corinthians 5:21 NIV**

Ciarra's Final Appeal

In my heart, I perceive that a problem lies in what fuels our drive to engage in spiritual growth. Being guilty of this myself at one point, I participated in prayer meetings, Bible study, and attended church frequently because I viewed it as what I *needed to do* in order to grow spiritually. As I truly gave my all to God and not just part of me, I learned that everything that I do should be driven by my delight in Jesus. The delight comes from first understanding how utterly hopeless and filthy my life has been without Him. Everything good that is present in my life is a direct result of God's grace and mercy. Once I realized that I could not trust myself, but I could trust Him, greater intimacy with Jesus Christ occurred. Now I approach situations differently, because my foundation with Him is solid. It is no longer tainted by my misconceptions of what I thought I should be or what I depicted love as being. My life is in complete oneness with Him who governs His will in and through my life. I finally found the complete fulfillment of my longing. I finally understand what it means to grow *in Him* and not just *with Him*.

Ponder Point: Our relationship with God must be one of constant repentance and cleansing so that we are prepared to worship Him, His holiness, and prepare our hearts as we draw near to Him in prayer. What people, places and things need to be dealt with in your life?

Reflections on the Path to Spiritual Maturity

My personal take-way from this chapter (what impacted me most):

_____

_____

Favorite quote from this chapter:

_____

_____

Area(s) covered that I am strongest in:

_____

_____

Area(s) covered that I need to grow in:

_____

_____

Scriptures and other resources to study (use for journaling and prayer):

_____

_____

_____

Who I will ask to hold me accountable (list the actions needed):

_____

_____

_____

Who I can help (share the lessons learned with others who need them):

_____

_____

_____

CHAPTER FOURTEEN

Accountability: Looking at Spiritual Growth through Your Own Eyes and Others

To become more accountable, you have to engage in constant renewal of your Spirit. By following His guidance and by honoring His Word, you are growing spiritually. Wise counsel from friends, who can give an accurate account of your life, is always helpful. If you are going to accept the counsel from others, you had better be holding yourself accountable as well.

The following are words from people in the Body of Christ sharing how Spiritual Growth has been applied to their lives and their relationships.

William Hardrick Jr. - *Entering a New Covenant*

Spiritual growth occurs when God is calling for more of you spiritually than you have experienced before. It is when you allow your views, prayers, and studies to expand you in a direction that reaches every way and still lead to God. I believe this begins to occur when you truly realize that your life is not your own, but that you were put on this earth for a reason. So when you or I are growing spiritually, we are stretched beyond our comfort and reshaped and reformed to what God has called us to be, and to live the life that He has called us to live. Spiritual growth is based on sacrifice. Simply the sacrificing of your life, for God's will for your life changes everything. In sacrificing my own will for God's will, I have learned I needed to let go of certain people. I've had a habit in life of attaching myself to people that don't pour into me, but allow me to pour into them. I have learned that a well can run dry, a lake can run dry but a river never runs dry as long as there is a stream pouring into it. I am learning in my life to allow God to make me a river where I can allow people to pour into me, so I can pour into others. I assure this by surrounding myself with people who are of open minds to whatever God is doing in them and in people around them. I indulge in positive affirmations daily and post scriptures and prayers around my house and job to reassure me that, no matter what, God will always stretch me, not to break me but to reform me.

Prayer, also, changed my reality. I realized that if you truly believe in the power of prayer, it can change your responses. I prayed years ago for God to make me into a man good enough to marry. God responded by showing me what women I shouldn't marry but had always invested time in. God also revealed the personal flaws that I needed to work on. Over time, I have learned that you can change your mind, but only God can change your heart. After I prayed for something different from God, He sent me the tools I needed to learn to become a better man. What God did in my life was teach me to be dedicated to something that will last for more than a few days. God began to put people in my life that would expose the things in me that I did not want to see. God can truly fix you if you give him all of your broken pieces. Therefore, I gave God all the pieces of my hate, love, hurt, pain, disappointment, rejection and fear for him to fix me. During this fixing process I learned so much about myself and about others. I learned that people need God. They need God's love and grace above anything else. The only way to give it to others is to experience it for yourself.

The personal re-forming God has done in my life is beautiful. It is reminiscent of a broken bone that healed wrong, so the doctors needed to re-break it for it to heal correctly. I thank Love – GOD - for showing me how to love. My spiritual growth has overflowed into every area of my life because it affects my heart. The physical heart is where the blood flows from. In essence, it is where life comes from. When God fixed my heart, He fixed the place where life comes from. My spiritual growth created in me a new life. In just a few months from the time of this writing, I will be getting married to a wonderful woman. I believed that God called her to my heart. My brain disagreed so initially I responded differently. I know now that my life began in my heart, where blood flows from. Therefore, my brain could only disagree so long because it can control my actions but cannot control the life that God has placed inside of me.

Growth or re-forming is an inevitable part of life. We can either grow taller in the things of God by having a strong foundation to stand upon or become fat in the things we eat and the sin we heavily indulge in. I thank God for Spiritual growth.

Taleka Anderson: *In the Waiting Period*

Spiritual Growth is when an individual understands that he or she must abide as the Bible states. In the beginning, Spiritual Growth can sometimes be difficult because human beings are accustomed to fitting in with the crowd. Sometimes we are placed inside the pit in order to gain proper focus. That way we can receive what it is that God has destined for us as His child.

Spiritual Growth requires life change decisions such as removal of certain individuals, loved ones or individuals labeled friends, simply because they are blocking our blessings. Once individuals remove themselves from the feelings of defeat, the blessings they once thought they were not able to receive begin to pour in overflow. Spiritual growth also requires change of life events such as rap music, explicit shows on television and movie screens. No, I am not saying you cannot *have a life* when it comes to spiritual growth but proper adjustments are required in order to *live fully*.

In my opinion, Spiritual Growth during the time of my last relationship didn't exist. I fought with someone who lied about being spiritually grounded. As the time went on, so much was revealed to me. He knew that I was then and am presently a spiritual individual, so his way of getting my attention was through pretending. He always found a reason that he couldn't attend church. I was so consumed with him and being a part of his zone that I would allow him to take up my scheduled space on Sundays with Christ and other spiritual practices. Looking back, I do not regret my last relationship because it was an *eye-opener* for me. Since I have removed myself from this relationship, I am happier.

Elree Cantry: *Divorced, but Not Forgotten*

Spiritual Growth is one's ability to review past experiences and decisions while truthfully accessing their measure of Christian standard of righteousness, or the lack thereof. All the while, one strives for a more intimate relationship with God through prayer, study, ministry, teaching, deeds, and faith as they continue their life's journey. The steps I am personally taking include daily prayer and conversation with Christ – having fewer conversations with man. I study the Word in places with the least amount of distractions so I can hear from the Lord. I try to listen to the Holy Spirit instead of always talking or asking God for things. Sometimes listening is the blessing and direction I need for my situation. I am active in ministry, exercising my faith and patience while performing deeds for others who may not be able to return the favor. My inner circle of people does not consist of perfect people, but they are people who are striving to obey God as well. I hold myself to a higher accountability and have a mindset that I may be the only Christian this person will ever meet. So I want to be the best disciple for Jesus Christ in order to point them in the direction of God the Father.

Spiritual Growth has made me realize that even though people may make me mad, lie or push my button, I realize I can't fall out with everybody. People have to come from the darkness into the light of Christ. God blessed me with a God-fearing mother and wonderful people throughout my life who blessed me in several ways. God *was* and *is* patient with me. Everyone grows at a different pace and in different seasons. If anyone is willing, they will grow to understand His will and eventually be able to truly love God, themselves and others.

My relationships with my co-workers, family members and friends have no drama. I don't partake in meaningless quarrels. Being right does not require for me to get out of character. Once married and now divorced, growing in Christ made me understand the importance of being evenly yoked. My need and desire is for a help mate and team member, not a trophy for bragging purposes. That does not mean my future wife will not be attractive. It means she will be beautiful - internally and externally. Most of all, my relationships are not based on what my needs or wants are from people. They are driven by what God wants me to do, learn, or receive as I interact with others. Even in negative situations with others, God is grooming and teaching me for His purpose - one that will bless me and others - now and later in life.

Donna King: *Covered by Restoration in her Remarriage - Nine Years of Marriage*

Spiritual growth is the process of moving from one realm of faith, wisdom, revelation, and power to the next. As baby Christians, you learn about salvation and etcetera. As you mature, your life begins to transform as a result of continuous study of the Word. It is applicable to your life when you commit to prayer and studying the Word on a daily basis. Your prayer time with God increases the amount of God that you walk in. For example, if you are constantly praying - then your attitudes, ways, thoughts, etc. should be a reflection of Him.

Daily, I ensure that spiritual growth is applied to my life by praying in the Holy Spirit. I may not always read my Word or devotion daily but I do pray in the Holy Ghost daily. This guides me in power, boldness, love, and faithfulness to a lifestyle pleasing to God. Because of this, I am more pleasant and Christ-like in my marriage. I honor my husband and serve in my home because doing so, first and foremost, pleases my Father. Before, as an immature Christian, I was very selfish as a wife and mother. Even though I am growing still, it reduces the amount of times I fail to walk in love or serve in my home.

Jonathan Macklin: *Waiting for his Rib*

My universal non-religious definition of Spiritual Growth is simply that it is a personal journey - mentally, physically, emotionally, and spiritually - in wisdom, knowledge, and understanding, for the sole purpose of building a stronger connection with the Creator for the fulfillment of one's created purpose. Spiritual Growth, which in my mind is different from Spiritual Maturity or Growing in Spiritual Maturity [a totally different conversation] is accomplished by first becoming a seeker of truth. This begins by first discovering who you are - not based upon what others may say or think about you, or defined by your accomplishments, mistakes, failures or achievements. No, Spiritual Growth is a journey of inwardly discovering how you are in your *inner man.* Spiritual Growth in its purest form is becoming comfortable with being defined by what God deposits in you. It is also developed through your individual experiences, your relationships, both on a personal and communal level. True spiritual growth is demonstrated by never settling or becoming satisfied with who you are or how things right now may define you, but always continually evolving taking on more Godlikeness.

Personally, it seems like mission impossible to truly stay faithful to my expectations and definition of spiritual growth. At times, I find it difficult not to allow life to distract me or even becoming complacent. What I try to live by is what even the Great Apostle Paul says he must do, "forget those things that are behind me reaching for those things that are before." I, like Paul, have to "press towards the mark of the prize of the High Calling which is in Christ Jesus." Literally, day by day, moment by moment, it seems I have to continually remind myself to stay focused, or just take the time and repent and get back on track. Every day it is necessary for me to pray for direction and enlightenment of who God says I am versus what my situation, people, or circumstances try to make me think I am. Again, I openly admit it is easy for me to become distracted and lose focus on a daily basis. What I try to do is hear God speaking in everything. Whether it be in my quiet time listening to music, working out, taking walks, reading my bible, studying, reading, hanging out with my homeboys, sons, family members, loved ones, or even through a dream. Whatever I am doing, I try to see God in it and make it part of my spiritual growth journey. I also utilize deep theoretical discussion, spiritual and intellectual conversations that challenge my beliefs and the way I previously viewed things. Along with attending church regularly or having political, religious, or financial discussions with people who might think or have a different background or belief system then mine is a way to challenge me to dig deeper.

One of the things I have learned in my spiritual growth journey is, two people can have the same experiences and be impacted differently by those experiences. They can even have two polar opposite recollections of those same experiences, based upon perception and individual perspective. As a result, on this journey I have learned to appreciate people for their differences and have developed a sense of understanding, tolerance, and forgiveness, there isn't much of anything I haven't or couldn't forgive someone. Now, this doesn't mean I'm willing to compromise my beliefs, desires, or even lower my expectation or standards. Quite the opposite, it is strengthening my resolve and persistence as it relates to relationships and what I expect, because I am learning to appreciate me and understand my worth. Just by my definition of *Spiritual Growth*, I am learning more and more daily. Everyone is not allowed to be a part of my life due to the purpose to which I was created and what I am to influence, and be influenced by. I have learned to look more introspectively at myself and discover who I really am. One of the lessons I am still learning is how to become better at allowing God to open and shut doors according to His Divine purpose without holding on too long or feeling guilty for letting go. As a result, I now see myself building healthier relationships that are not so one-sided, stressful and destructive. This journey is far from over. Yet, I see myself becoming a better human being, father, friend, and future husband. My *Spiritual Growth* in the last 24 months has taught me patience and more importantly, how to patiently wait on God to perform according to His word and not my own desires, lust, or expectations.

Roseann Mattocks: *Joined as ONE for 15 Years*

Spiritual growth to me just means becoming more like Christ every day - showing evidence of the fruit of the Spirit, living in his will, and becoming more trusting of him leading and guiding my life in *all* things. This is applicable to my life in very practical ways, such as treating others with love and respect, even when love and respect is not given to me, or even when my views, beliefs and morals are different from theirs. Christ has commissioned me to love everyone. Living in His will does not mean that I do everything right all of the time, it simply expresses the desire to do what He would have me to do. I want to be in God's will so I ask for His will to be done in my life. From that moment on, I do not have to worry. He will impress on my mind and my heart to do the right things. When I do wrong, it is because I have exerted my will against my Heavenly Father's in a fight for control. This leads me to my last spiritual growth point, which is trusting God to lead my life in all things. This one is the most difficult for me. However, I know that because God knows the end from the beginning, it is imperative that He receives the reins to my life in order for me to live in His will. This means that even when things look like they are not working out in the way I think they should, I should continue to pray for strength to continue to trust Him instead of taking the reins and trying to control the outcome myself. These things are challenging evidences of spiritual growth. They do not always happen at the same time, nor do they happen every day - or in this order. But as long as there is a concerted effort every day to *die to self* and allow God to take control of every aspect of our lives, spiritual growth will be there.

The following steps I have taken to ensure spiritual growth in my marriage are as follows: accepting God's salvation for me, staying in the Word of God, and constantly, consistently praying, asking Him to help me to empty myself so that He can fill me up with His Holy Spirit. Also included is allowing my husband and me to admit when we are wrong and apologize for it. This includes laying down ego and the need to be right. We are always able to treat each other with love and respect, even when we disagree. Just like God has unselfishly given His all for us, we must be willing to do this for the ones to which we have committed our lives.

Reflections on Your *Growing Painz* and Points to Ponder

1. **What is your definition of Spiritual Growth and how can it be applied to your life?**

    _____

    _____

    _____

    _____

    _____

2. **What steps are you taking to ensure Spiritual Growth is applied to your life?**

    _____

    _____

    _____

    _____

    _____

3. **How has Spiritual Growth enhanced your relationships?**

    _____

    _____

    _____

    _____

    _____

Reflections on the Path to Spiritual Maturity

My personal take-way from this chapter (what impacted me most):

_____

_____

Favorite quote from this chapter:

_____

_____

Area(s) covered that I am strongest in:

_____

_____

Area(s) covered that I need to grow in:

_____

_____

Scriptures and other resources to study (use for journaling and prayer):

_____

_____

_____

Who I will ask to hold me accountable (list the actions needed):

_____

_____

_____

Who I can help (share the lessons learned with others who need them):

_____

_____

_____

AFTERWORD

As you read ***Growing Painz***, I pray and hope you were encouraged and are ready for growth. As you continue to press forward in your walk, hold on to God and know that your strength comes from Him. God sees your suffering, hurts, and pains. Everything you've been through or are currently going through, He sees. He is with you in the midst of it all. You may not see Him working, but He is, and sooner than later, your purpose will be revealed.

The Father wants you to find strength in Him through every obstacle you face. It is easy to get discouraged, but through prayer and trusting in Him, God promises to be with you always. As you pray, remember that provision has already been made. You are simply waiting patiently for the One who know you, loves you, hears you, and is molding you into *His image*.

Remember, love covers a multitude of sins. Jesus demonstrated that when He died for you. Human nature is flawed but as you draw closer to God, He'll continue to show you oneness with Him. In His covering, there is no judgment, but love, peace, forgiveness, unity, and **GROWTH**. Attacks will come, but your weapon is a sword that reads:

God's vessel once tainted but now *free*.

Message to All: Although you're in a spiritual battle every day and sin is accepted by society, you have assurance the war has already been won. You do not have to be paralyzed by sin; you can overcome sin through Christ. (1 John 3:8-AMP)

Whatever you focus on, you will become. Your emotions will soon take over, and your thoughts will soon become a craving desire that you will likely follow (**sin**). Get your eyes off your flesh (**sin**) and look toward your healing...this will be your *Growing Painz.*

> *That you may walk (live and conduct yourselves) in a manner worthy of the Lord, fully pleasing to Him and desiring to please Him in all things, bearing fruit in every good work and steadily growing and increasing in and by the knowledge of God (with fuller, deeper, and clearer insight, acquaintance, and recognition).*
>
> ***Colossians 1:10 AMP***

ABOUT THE AUTHOR

Ciarra S. Leathers is the author of *Season of Singleness*. She is an inspiring Woman of God and encourager. She is known for her Godly lifestyle and transparent attitude. She is originally from Kansas City, Missouri, but resides in Houston, Texas.

Her successes have led her to be an inspiration to others. Throughout the triumphs she has faced in her own life, she has been able to touch and inspire others with her story. Ciarra has a passion to reach troubled youth and women in the faith. She has been a counselor and encourager to many who have crossed her path. She is equipped to bring out the best in women and motivate them into a deeper connection with God.

Ciarra holds a Masters in Counseling from Houston Graduate School of Theology. She also holds a Bachelors of Arts in English with a concentration in Journalism from Missouri Western State University in Saint Joseph, Missouri.

Ciarra currently counsels troubled youth. Her mission is to reach everyone with the Gospel of Christ, exposing the enemy while glorifying the Kingdom of God. Her heart-felt desire is that everyone will walk in the likeness of Christ.

To contact the author for encouragement, speaking engagements, and other requests, please contact her via email at **Jesusluvsme_13@msn.com**

Also connect with Author Ciarra Leathers at:
Website: www.ciarraleathers.com
Twitter: @AuthorCiarraL
Facebook: Author Ciarra Leathers
IG: @authorciarral

APPENDIX

Frequently Asked Questions

Growing in God in The Midst of Chaos

1. Can you still trust after infidelity?

Yes, but if will be difficult. It will take time to rebuild the trust that was lost. As you believe in God and trust in His goodness, no matter how long it will take, the trust can be restored. For a person to admit their mistakes opens the door to forgiveness and restoration of the relationship. The steps you have to go through in your healing: *Denial, Realization, Anger,* and *Forgiveness.* Once you've experienced these steps, you have been healed. Love can win, and forgiveness does work, but you have to be willing-*Sacrifice.*

2. Why do people cheat?

Women cheat to fill a void from something they are missing or from unresolved past issues. Men cheat because they can. No one is immune to cheating. Once you believe you are- you fail. We are born sinners, unrighteous, and flawed. In His blood we are made right with God, so through Him we find faithfulness. Through Him we find loyalty. It is not in our own efforts but through constant renewal and dying to flesh, we can truly be faithful.

Note to men: Shower her with compliments, love, attention, and affection. Show her that your heart is in it, and no man can compare.

Note to women: Show support, uplifting, honoring, and respecting your spouse. Show him that it will be difficult for another woman to fill her shoes.

3. Should I have faith that my desire for marriage will be fulfilled?

God knows the desires of your heart and would not place that desire there if it wasn't going to happen. I think we often lose focus on the need to please, serve, and attend to Him. All else will be added, if we are patient with Him. Exercise your faith and remember His timing is not ours. When you least expect a mate, he or she will be placed in your life. The proper time may not be now. Today, you must focus on this *season of growth*. Growing and becoming a better person for not only yourself but your future spouse.

4. How do you become content with not being in a relationship?

You have to be content with the vision God has placed in your heart. Through prayer and much needed time with the Lord. Focus on your eagerness to please Him, rather than your eagerness to please your flesh. In order to be all you can be for your spouse, you have to first submit your all to Him.

5. Why is it not safe to jump into another relationship after one ends?

You will be doing yourself a disservice and the person you are with. It is not wise to enter another relationship before properly healing from the last one. You know yourself with someone and not alone, so you would never know if you are with that person based on love or fear of being alone. The unresolved issues from the last relationship will start to affect your current relationship. The proper way to heal is with the guidance of God. Healing takes time. Heal alone - first.

6. How long should I wait and how do I know he or she is the one?

You wait until, God tells you otherwise. If someone is trying to convince you to rush and it contradicts what God has told you, be assured that person is not the one. The peace that comes upon you should assure you that person is the one. You should not have to get reassurance.

- If he or she is not motivated about the growth of the relationship- They are not the one.
- If you have shown him or her more attention than they have shown you, he or she is not the one.

7. Why have no sex before marriage?

Sex was intended to bring two people together as one in a marriage union. Sex before marriage distorts your perception of love within a union. It causes you to think and act based on emotions rather than the reality of God's spiritual order. Your decisions to stay would solely be based on the physical pleasure of the relationship. Sex should not be the glue that holds you two together.

8. If God loves me, why do I have so much chaos in my life?

Sometimes things we experience are consequences of the decisions we make. The best way to learn from your mistakes is to suffer the ramifications of your actions. Remember, there is a purpose for every chaotic situation you go through. While you think it's hurting you, it is actually helping you heal.

9. How can I grow in God?

We grow in God by acknowledging our need for salvation and forgiveness. By seeking to know Him deeply, His love will become more and more familiar to us.

10. What are some things I should do to discover God's love?

The best way to experience God's love is to let go and allow God to work in your life. We may learn more about His love and how to love others by allowing Him to work out His purpose for our lives.

PRAYERS

Jesus taught His disciples that prayer is an expression of an intimate relationship with God, who makes His love available to you. As you pray, you seek God with all your heart. This act of prayer shows you are vulnerable and ready to be forgiven through your act of repentance. Prayer is spent in the presence of God. Remember, prayer is more than simply asking God what you want Him to fix. It is living in obedience and trusting in Him to see you through. You will fall and have not so great days, but provision comes when we are in constant pursuit of His will and not your own.

> *Lord, I wait for you; you will answer, Lord my God. . . . I confess my iniquity; I am sorry for what I have done.*
> **Psalm 38:15, 18 NIV**

The following prayers are prayers anyone can use to be delivered from their struggle. They're listed by a particular struggle and this does not mean you are restored but it is steps toward your healing and restoration. It is important to cry out to the Lord in prayer because it's a form of worship by humility. You can be confident of God's response to your prayers when you submit first in prayer.

Adulterous Spirit

Dear Heavenly Father, I really do not understand how you continue to see me worthy when I am filth. I continue to let my flesh push me in ways my spirit is not willing to follow. I ask you to deliver me from this adulterous spirit and place upon me a faithful spirit. I know I have to be faithful in my commitment I made you, so I can be faithful in my relationship. I know I will not change overnight, but through your help I can make progress every day. I want to honor you with my body and show you I am willing to do my part. Today, I am submitting myself to you and dying to the old me, so I can become a better person for myself and in my relationship. In Jesus name I pray, Amen!

Going Through a Divorce and Praying for Restoration

Dear Heavenly Father, my heart is in need of restoration in my marriage. I know you have the power to restore my marriage where we both went wrong. I believe in your Word, your voice, and your continued faithfulness in my life. I believe in the covenant of marriage, and that you honor marriage. I know I am unable to restore my marriage myself, so I am completely giving you total control of restoring my marriage. Lord, I want You to take the wheel as I sit back and trust you. I believe what your Word says, about marriage, and how You frown upon divorce. The covenant of marriage is a lifelong union and the fulfillment of something great. I no longer trust in my own strength, because I know I am weak without you. Through this period I will remain focused on you while you continue to work on my spouse and me. In Jesus' name I pray, Amen!"

Dealing with Lust

Dear Heavenly Father, I no longer want to thirst for another person. I want to thirst for you, my soul needs you. I want this unwanted spirit of lust to leave. Each day I want to renew my heart, mind, and body to you. I want to free myself from the bondage of lust that lurks in me. Cleanse me from this sin and purify my heart. I no longer want this to dictate my actions. I know if I resist the enemy and his tactics he will flee from me. I am calling on your name Father; I am covered in your grace, and made right with your blood. In Jesus' name I pray, Amen!

Fear of Being Lonely

Dear Heavenly Father, thank you for wanting to pursue me and hold me. Thank you for seeing me as worthy when I consider myself unworthy. Please forgive me for the times I allowed someone else to take the place of you in my life. Protect me from the feeling of being alone and unloved, when I know you love and cherish me. Help me to be content with your presence in my life and not someone else. Only you can fulfill the void of my loneliness. Only you can love me like no one else. I truly long for you, cover me, and keep me. In Jesus' name I pray, Amen!

Growing in Discipline

Dear Heavenly Father, I cast out every stronghold that is interfering with my growth process. I want to continue to walk in your Will. Trusting and believing in your direction. I want to find peace in you. I cannot do it on my own, I need to reconcile myself to you daily, and ask you to forgive my sins, and make me clean in your sight. I know that sin breaks my relationship with You. So, as I confess my sins and move in faith, I know that over time my life will resemble yours. Even through my moments of doubt, I will invest the effort and discipline to allow my faith to **grow**. *In Jesus' name I pray, Amen!*

ACCEPTANCE

Acceptance is admitting you need a Savior to be cleansed of your sins. To move forward with salvation, you no longer have your sins counted against you, but are forgiven through God's grace and mercy. Salvation is available to all who believe in Jesus Christ. Christ himself promised that those who believe in Him will be saved. If you haven't accepted Christ in your life, today is the day.

How to Come to Christ

- Confess your sins. Repent of your sins. Turn away from them. Transform, renew your mind and change your way of thinking. (Acts 3:19)
- Ask Jesus Christ, the Son of God to come into your life and believe in God who sent Christ to earth for all of us. (John 3:16; John 5:24)
- Confess Jesus Christ as Lord and Savior of your life. Nothing or anyone else can save you and pay the price needed to redeem you from a life of sin and separation from God. (Romans 10:9-13)

OTHER BOOKS
BY CIARRA LEATHERS

Season of Singleness

Every little girl longs for a relationship with her father. Sadly, when the father is absent, it leaves a deep hole in the heart of the woman she becomes. The search for love never ends.

Season of Singleness is a heartfelt story about one little girl who grew up without the guidance of a father. Throughout his absence in her life, she began to search for his love in other men. Over time and many hardships, she realized the kind of love she was searching for could only be found in One source. Jesus Christ was her answer to love, forgiveness and acceptance. Finally, she came to know God as the Father she always longed for. In her relationship with Him, she found strength to endure and overcome, discernment to help her make wise choices, and wisdom to live life wholly.

www.ingramcontent.com/pod-product-compliance
Lightning Source LLC
Chambersburg PA
CBHW052112090426

42741CB00009B/1784